# Lost & Found

*poems by*

# Joann Deiudicibus

*Finishing Line Press*
Georgetown, Kentucky

# Lost & Found

## ACKNOWLEDGMENTS

With thanks to the editors of the following publications, in which some of
these poems first appeared, some in earlier forms:

*Calling All Poets Twentieth Anniversary* Anthology 2020: "Against Dawn"
*Chronogram*: "Gone"
*Comstock Review*: "Notes for New Writers," "Forecast," "Last Call"
*Contemporary Haibun Online*, 19.3: "Duplex"
*Drifting Sands,* Issue 21: "Echolocation"
*Poetry Quarterly*: "Family Portrait"
*Reflecting Pool: Poets and the Creative Process*: "First Snow," "Survivor's Guilt"
*Shawangunk Review*: "Afterward," "Lost and Found," "Origin Story"
"Survivor's Guilt," "Taboo," "The Geography of Grief," "Things that Have
Nothing to do with Grief"
*A Slant of Light: Contemporary Women Writers of the Hudson Valley*:
"Birthmark"
*Stone Poetry Quarterly*: "Angel of Constellations," "At Home"
*Typishly*: "Swimming"


Publisher: Leah Huete de Maines
Editor: Christen Kincaid
Cover Art: Steven McLellan, Creative Director & Owner of Garden Delights
Fine Florist
Author Photo: Christopher Wheeling, Poet & Photographer
Cover Design: Elizabeth Maines McCleavy


Order online: www.finishinglinepress.com
also available on amazon.com

Author inquiries and mail orders:
Finishing Line Press
PO Box 1626
Georgetown, Kentucky 40324
USA

# Contents

*For Thomas Festa*

Let me abide in your shadow—
let me hold on
to the edge of your robe
as you determine
what you must let be lost
and what will be saved.

"Maker of All Things, Even Healings"
                    —Mary Oliver

## Notes for New Writers

Let the only liars you trust be poets.
Let what's earthly be afterlife,
mud caked boots uprooted in spring.
Let absence fill you like blue flames
until silence devours your margins.
The silence of chaos tells nothing
as the silence of everything listens.
Like the trees, bear witness.
Hold these sounds with out-
stretched leaves. Can you speak
in song? Will you make
a picture of God, birthed
from your heart-throat,
cut from light, carved
by breath that blooms
in blood? May your body
be a poem: furrow and field,
everything in between
the lines—fresh waters,
paths of fallen fruit
rotting sweetly,
feeding what grows.

## Against Dawn

*In response to "Double Rape, Lynching in India Exposes Caste Fault Lines" by Julie McCarthy*

It's been said that for mangoes red does not mean ripe.
Why then did they take you from that tree, age 12,
only to tie you back to its branches? Torn
fruit cannot be returned by its stem to its root.
Didn't they squeeze gently and feel you were not ready?
Couldn't they judge by touch that your cousin was, too,
green at age 14—flesh pressing against thumbs in protest.
The aroma of womanhood had not yet infused the fields of your bodies.
In this place, mint, dung, and ash tour the nostrils,
casting a noxious concoction of sweet necrosis.
How you dangled there from fallopian branches,
paisley eggs fashionably sashed, swaying alongside leaves.
"And when they cannot control us, they kill us,"
a woman said. To be suspended by men
is the only way to reach their height:
a dream of weightless feet floating against dawn.

## Survivor's Guilt

*Prepare yourself.*
Prepare your shoeless feet for paths
scattered with stone, shells, bone-shatter, casings.

There will be flowers,
stems bound like limbs,
bunches of legs dangling above water;
flowers pulled from fields,
dug from torn ground, rootless.

There will be blood-black blooms,
mud-colored hair spilling like petals,
dark shards arranged in sharp angles.

Those chosen could not prepare:
Captives cast off like chaff
or thrown atop pyres,
stalks askew, barbed leaves lifting
like ash-flecked palms in prayer.

*Prepare yourself.*
The rampart about your heart bursting with grief,
as shrapnel seeps into tight red bud.

## The Geography of Grief

He moved windward
from New York tenement
to farmhouse where
he learned the solitary hike.
Later, he'd trek international,
orienteer with his nephew.

He and the boy had just been sledding.
Frozen still: their feet printing
a path home in snow until
he moved ahead alone
to meet his cartographer.

The annual thaw charts his
departure in alluvial pools—
water always abandons.

## Origin Story

*After Joy Harjo*

Remember the last breath should be as full as the first.
Know each of your lung's landscapes.
Remember each cut as well as each kiss.
Know that every touch on your body marks a path back to love.
Remember day-break and wave-break; map points
where they burst over and inside of your metronomic heart,
siphoning shores of that abandoned island.
Remember you are salt and sand, star and seaweed,
seed and skeleton, a sound tsunami
cresting at the speed of light.
Remember that the mother who bore you also shattered,
the father that failed you also made you.
Your eyes may be bright with a prophet's vision,
your hair may burn pale as the moon, but
remember the belly that bred you, the hands
that raised you up, skyward where you could almost
reach what had ripened, taste the air like Eve,
who, uncoiling from some cosmic conch,
was called womb-ward from the waves.
Remember her voice speaking in serpentine tongues,
how she bled sin to sing you, her first hymn.

## Last Call

*"If you go through / there is always the risk /
of remembering your name"* —*Adrienne Rich*

It wasn't that I didn't want to
tell you, but the world split open
and the words did not come;
the sound for s-t-o-p suddenly silenced
somewhere deep in mind, drowned
at the source, broken bucket
at the bottom of a well, abandoned bailer.
I never knew how to name what hid
in the dark places, my need born edging
shadow and light. From the moment
they took me from you, two
cleaved from one—that final call
echoed familiar from maternity ward halls.
The nurses said it can only be one of
a few things: hunger, exhaustion, shit.
Who can ask for something
they don't yet know, have no
words for: milk, blood, breast? Mother,
who can say where any of us belong?
My voice like my names changed.
Give me time, I screamed,
ringing in your ears,
but you split open,
fractured flower,
giving me up to the world.

## Taboo

In thirty-four years, I was born and you died twice.
At birth, Catholic charities sent you to live upstate
with silence and faces that look nothing like you.

Incubator womb, oxygen tube, jaundice,
four pounds: I took seven months to cultivate.
In thirty-four years, I was born and you died twice.

In a barn, on feed bags infested with mice,
my father took you. The jaws of life extricate
your silence and faces that look nothing like you.

The suckling denied breast still grew.
Mothers mourn the empty house's weight.
In thirty-four years, I was born and you died twice.

Still, I pick up your unfamiliar voice
calling like an old psalm. What's akin alienates:
Silence and faces that look nothing like you.

One labored, the other raised and gave advice.
Only a child of two tribes can relate.
In thirty-four years, I was born but both died twice—
in silence with faces that look something like you.

## Family Portrait

The home that warmed you after that long trip down
from the Canadian border, where Catholic Charities
hoarded babies—for those without—to pick like flowers.

The small, blue house where you peered into windows
that creak and whistle in winter, unlocked
cabinets your father built to store memories.

The china closet in the dining room, where
your mother's Polish tchotchkes still stand at attention
among her mother's dishes, an homage to order.

He, a woodworker, she, a nurse, took you and the boy
when you were just toddlers. Though you shared
no blood, you became one another's keepers.

In this photo, you are only a teenager,
sitting prettily in a blue dress to match
your smiling eyes, father beside.

Your brother's dark hair, your blonde waves
warmed by your mother's chestnut coif—
soon you'd be kicked out of the picture.

Yet brother was the one they could not keep for long:
He fled in his twenties unexpectedly hemorrhaging
under skull. No one anticipated aneurysm.

Now, a woman in your fifties you live alone,
having survived the war of parentlessness
twice, one more thing we have in common.

But the burden of the house—leaks that
feed foreclosure in an IV drip, stretch marks
in cement steps etched with ice—is too much labor.

When the snow comes to cover us
in its quiet, everything will still, frozen
gutters glittering, unanswered questions.

What you mean to ask is not if the house
still stands to the elements.
For all that you've lost is greater than this

one small, blue house that cannot hold
your father's last words, your mother's confession
over homemade latkes, or her best advice:

That you offer me to those without,
to be picked like a flower the way she
and your father picked you and your brother.

What you need to ask but cannot is this:
Am I still here if I cannot be within those walls
with the only ones I have known as my own.

## Birthmark

We talk of cleaning the rugs, under
the rugs, and suddenly
I enter into another childhood
like the cat I dropped off in the town
where I was born
one hour from home.
I have found my way here.
I know the face of the strange woman
who gave birth to me in St. Anthony's.
I don't know this blue house
but remember our eyes, their right angles,
each a tidy room with torn-screen centers:
and her dyed blonde hair
curling tightly like a daughter's fist
about her mother's finger.

## Echolocation

My mother gave nothing away, still does. She tried to teach me not to be afraid—though in the dark woods surrounding the two-story, white Victorian—lurked all that was unknown. Brush-rustle. Twig-snap. Invisible limbs waiting to snatch me back to a home without lilacs, a pet cemetery, or swimming pool, a home without memory where a woman I'd never known claimed to remember me. When July lightning suddenly flickered, scarring the night sky, my mother would stay inside, hide her eyes. I'd run straight to the porch swing, seek open sky, afraid to blink and miss a flash. Both of us holding our breath. Everything starless now glittered— raindrops on grass and window glass.

peeper song silenced
heart thunder
ready to strike

**Lost & Found**

A dead letter box of lonely earrings,
stuffed animals, keys with attachment issues.

Silent telephone wires that spark
occasional, one-way conversations.

A daily psalm—groceries, bills, call mom—
crumpled in the pocket of laundered jeans.

The turn-around, look-everywhere prayer
to St. Anthony, an elegy to memory.

## The Rocking

*For Emmett Till (Photograph by David Jackson,*
*Jet Magazine 1955)*

That boy, fourteen and flirty,
shored the load, all 75 pounds,
all the way to the riverbank.
Stripped of his father's smile,
but never was his daddy. That boy
beneath blankets of blackness
had silver stainless wheels to deliver
*him unto death for Christ's sake.*

That boy's blessed face, taken into
the river's hands, its blackness
washed to the near-white of sand,
holy robes of skin undone,
doctored by the rock of waters.
*All who live will be delivered to Him.*

Flathead catfish and black bass
rowed him after the undertow
of fists, those boys' barbs and bullet.
Three sinking summer suns till
he'd rise miraculous from mussel bed,
*that He may be manifest.*

When they brought him home,
his mother said, I won't get any
help carrying this load. Brother
beside steeled her at the viewing:
all rifle gaze with blind aim.
*All who live will be delivered to Him.*

She tucked in her boy one
more time rocking him off,
his body empty as a milk bottle.
At the funeral, folks tried on
his child size, cribbed his build

in plain sight: too tight to breathe in,
too dark to leave alone.
*God in the face of Christ.*

Money, claim your Tallahatchie Blues,
your crappies, our dead dropping
into this deep. Name him, slack kin,
that boy pitched and plunged into
Black Bayou—baptized by buckshot,
still floating free in these waters.

## Angel of Constellations

When you woke  I was gone
strange stars fixed
me in pooling darkness
light slipping  tossed under and up
floating back to surface-
less wave-swell
I awoke to undertow
you to solitude  the near silence
of machines breathing
and I—empty bellied angel of light—
showed you the way    *this* way
yes   this is the way to heaven   step
by step   falling down   into
cold   blue   sky

## Duplex

My mother's apartment in the town where I grew up burned in 2014. Later, the trend caught on with other Victorian homes grandfathered in without inspection. The old brick building's attic already breathed must and smoke—filled with singed relics: a wooden trunk, antique jars and bottles, odd clippings and ends. The adjoining attorney's office was wall-stacked with jaundiced newspapers, gold-trimmed books, yellow legal pads and Post-its. Mechanical failure (crossed wires) or act of nature (a gnawing squirrel)? Cause and origin unknown.

When I got the call, I thought maybe she'd fallen asleep smoking in bed, or that one of her Yankee candles or incense sticks got knocked over by the cats. But my mother was at work managing the small drug store that's since gone out of business. Our side of the building still intact suffered mostly smoke damage. Water cracked and peeled the pink walls of the bedroom we once shared. Photos in fractured glass frames fell with ash from shattered windows onto small patches of grass and concrete. Things were gutted. My mother would have to move. A fireman saved one cat, but the other's body was never found. A friend picked me up. My mind wandered; its eye fixed on childhood marks—the only way home.

bomb peonies flashing
through the graveyard gate
a deer corpse opens

## Gone

February flakes its tarry roof
in a burning blizzard of shingle
ash, singed pages, and
melted tools for calculating
some infinite amount that cannot
be made to cover the cost of living.

This is what life becomes:
business. The active rush from
rise, like a steep pitched attic
touching the lawless sky
to fall as smoke-sallow leaves
to the ground, where everything
comes to lie.

## Dura Mater

No drink in decades, yet
the headaches throbbed through
her days like bruised hangovers.
MRI showed dural mass with flare sign,
tail like a comet flashing at the base of the skull.

A gnarled pit, once slow-motion,
now swelled at the speed of light,
pressing cranial nerves, disordering the senses:
a dimming hum, the dizzying dance of meteors
falling to the beat of their own bright music.

Times between appointments
you avoided words like tumor,
craniotomy, radiation: the silence
of miles between your bodies.

The cells grew like you had in her,
umbilically bound to their host.
Posterior fossa, mother of movement,
balance, and breath became strange-
faced family, entangled kin.

Then, a breakthrough to soft center,
the seed of being, bone opening to a drill's hiss.
Left behind, you could only wonder,
Where do we go when we go
under delirious tides in bloom?

Ragdoll-stitched, she'd wake anew
to dark bud plucked from stem,
aster from disaster.
Doctor's orders: Recall nothing.

## Swimming

The man next door is useful.
He mows around our shed in spring, cuts
firewood, stacking it smartly for winter.
His wife comes outside only in morning,

shuffles down the driveway, crossing the road
to the mailbox. She is pale as an ocean
stone with sand-scraped skin
softened by the circling sea.

Now, it is summer. Her husband
skims the in-ground pool.
For hours, he stands over nearly-
clear water removing debris.

He never stops skimming, skips
breakfast, work, phone calls, dessert.
The grass grows high against the shed.
The lawn stretches lazily as the wind yawns.

The mailbox shuts its mouth:
it is full of unanswered statements.
The man next door skims
the surface of the unused pool.

He catches leaves, Polly noses, Japanese beetles.
At night, he dreams of quarantine: black
iridescent blotches, Rorschach
butterflies floating into white net.

## Things that Have Nothing to Do with Grief

I.
I pull her red corduroy jacket
around me like the blanket my mother
crocheted for our first apartment.

II.
Fingernails split like
petals of dried orchids.

## How to Stop a Runaway Horse

Easy now, tell her,
your bridled fire.
Be calm, but firm.
Sit up. Tits out. Heels down.
She's buzzing, but don't
lose your balance,
your mind. Find a circle.
Bend the neck to slow her
legs. Entangle fingers in mane.
Find synchronized time.
The unbroken horse
learns to pull,
wants to set pace, bucks:
bone-crack booming
under hoof.
More hurricane
than horse, she is
darkening weather.
Once, she almost broke
me, breaking into canter,
but my hands, numb and
bloodied, held tight.

## Forecast

The flower moon bewitches waves,
lifts surf without strings, as white-
cap melodies drown sound.
We beat the sun for one short walk
in lunar light. Meanings tangle up in lines,
tendrilled beams blooming arterial. We are
bound newly to this world by strange weather,
silver threads stitched together by tides:
Learning the geography of scars, anatomy's alchemy,
learning the language of riptide tongues.
Chasing storm under cloud cover, in darkness
bright I enter the eye, and wait—skinless
hands upturned and reaching
to touch your torrents, fall to surge, inhale
this undertow, become the deluge.

## At Home

Today the house is quiet, filled with work,
things that creak or drip, that ding softly—
reminders of how to avoid the self, soothe the self.

You are gone, and I am alone.
Light pours in warming winter windows like
the cups of your hands that heat my feet this February.

Today I am not lonely but feel the peace
of emptiness, the longing for your voice
as deep and warm as the womb we're without,

the home behind us that we cannot hold, but
reach to remake, paint, decorate, fill needlessly.
Today, you fill me with need, with words

that must speak, sing sorrows of what
broke in us and what we shattered:
The parents that wrinkle and fade,

the children unborn or scheduled to die
without our knowledge of when, only that.
Today, I need to fill everything that I cannot

see, pressing into the dark corners and crawl-
spaces of memory—boxed vases, hand-
stitched quilts, flannel shirts, blotched photos.

Today, I keep time by a watch worn yesterday,
feel this afternoon light for what comes next,
ordering tomorrow for a house we've never met.

Now, we're miles from mothers, farthest from fathers.
But when the weather turns against us,
we'll wait out the hours.

## Kept

What named us strange, mother?
Who uttered us into this life, then dug us up with forked tongues.
We furious flowers left to odd lands, called by another name:
stargazers whose rootedness would not take.
What little did we know except we were born to hunger?
Lilies, too, mirror and multiply, lifting awaited faces toward sky.
Left alone, tubers twin as life performs its parlor trick again and again.
It takes a river of stars to make a galaxy and one electrostatic bolt to
    birth a god.
You named me blessing at first sight. I named you ray of light
but called you refraction. Yet etchings inscribe who
we thought we were. Free of flesh, we wish there were no secrets left.
Mother, I'm calling for answers caught
in history's throat, cut to bear the labor of language.
Dubbed bastards at birth, we've gone
by our Latin names, epithets, aliases—
anything to be known.

## Open Letter to a Daughter

Let the world unfurl
its small paw in the palm
of your hand, stretch
into that space, flex
claw into tender flesh.
Let its hallelujah blue hold
you in, stir sudden winds
too wild to catch—feather-fall
from unsure heavens.
Let it mark you, sharp-
toothed, call you by name,
etch swirling constellations
into your skin—fingerprints
of the invisible infinite.

Somedays, it may hold
its breath, hunched in the corner,
fix on you its slitted eye.
The world has trust issues,
you know. It's never had
a good home, its own family.
Sure, it's learned to survive
its kill. Still, we tried to teach it
to sing with a mouthful of quills.
Let the world be, as you will
be—heavy light radiating matter—
purring its rhythmic, jagged love.

## With Thanks

With deep gratitude to those who offered thoughts on these poems, who gave them time and a place—Laurence (Larry) Carr, Mike Jurkovic, Amanda Russell, Guy Reed, Phillip X Levine, Raphael Kosek, Jan Schmidt, Ken Holland, Susan Chute, Timothy Liu, Lucia Cherciu, and the late Harry Stoneback. With love and admiration for the late Pauline Uchmanowicz, poet, teacher, mentor, and friend, whose belief has steadied my voice.

**Joann Deiudicibus** teaches writing in New York's Hudson Valley. Her poems and essays about poetry appear in *WaterWrites: A Hudson River Anthology* (coeditor); *A Slant of Light: Contemporary Women Writers of the Hudson Valley;* and *Reflecting Pool: Poets and the Creative Process* (Codhill Press), as well as in *Comstock Review, Blithe Spirit, Contemporary Haibun Online, Drifting Sands, Typishly, Stone Poetry Quarterly, The Shawangunk Review (current poetry guest editor), Calling All Poets Anthologies, Chronogram,* and *Lightwood.* Joann's essay, "Axing the Frozen Sea: Female Inscriptions of Madness," an analytical and personal exploration of mental health's effects on the works of Anne Sexton, Linda Gray Sexton, and Marya Hornbacher appears in the anthology *Affective Disorder and the Writing Life* (Palgrave Macmillan). Ask her about true crime, cats, and confessionalism.